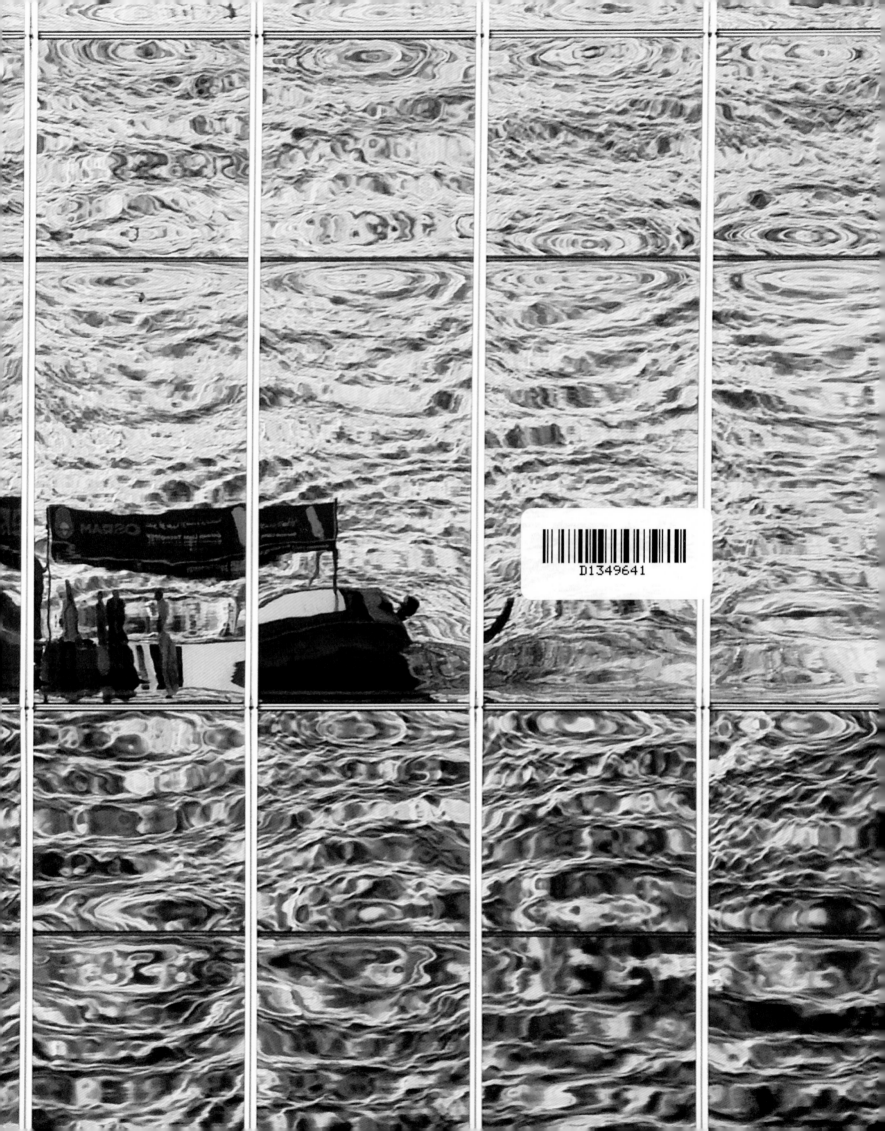

Dubai
A City Portrait

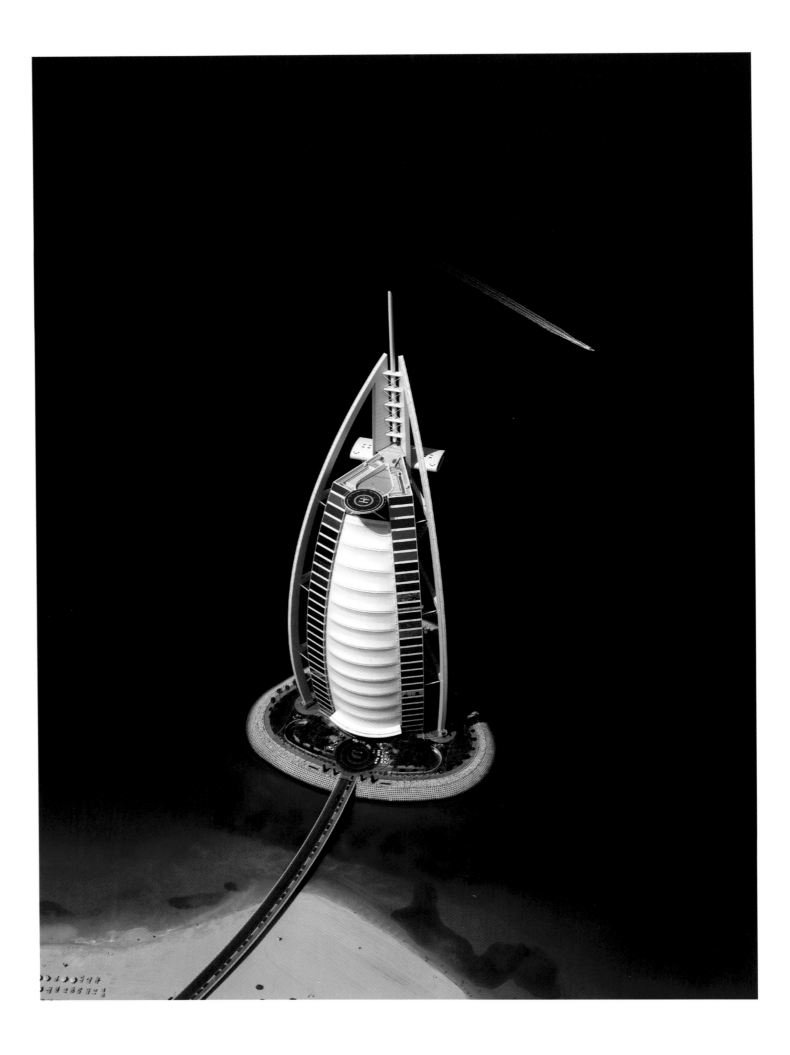

Dubai

A City Portrait

Patrick Lichfield

MOTIVATE
PUBLISHING

Published by Motivate Publishing

Dubai: PO Box 2331, Dubai, UAE
Tel: (+971) 4 282 4060, fax: (+971) 4 282 0428
e-mail: books@motivate.ae   www.booksarabia.com

Office 508, Building No 8, Dubai Media City, Dubai, UAE
Tel: (+971) 4 390 3550, fax: (+971) 4 390 4845

Abu Dhabi: PO Box 43072, Abu Dhabi, UAE
Tel: (+971) 2 627 1666, fax: (+971) 2 627 1566

London: Acre House, 11/15 William Road, London NW1 3ER
e-mail: motivateuk@motivate.ae

Directors: Obaid Humaid Al Tayer and Ian Fairservice

Editorial Director: Ian Fairservice
Senior Editor: David Steele
Editor: Pippa Sanderson
Assistant Editor: Zelda Pinto
Senior Designer: Andrea Willmore
Book Publishing Manager: Jeremy Brinton

ISBN: 1 86063 166 5

British Library Cataloguing-in-Publication Data. A catalogue record for this
book is available from the British Library.

Printed by Emirates Printing Press, Dubai, United Arab Emirates

FRONT COVER: Dhows on Dubai Creek.
HALF-TITLE PAGE: Portrait of a Bedouin.
TITLE PAGE: Burj Al Arab, an icon of Dubai.
IMPRINT PAGE: The beach at Madinat Jumeirah.
BACK COVER: At work on the dunefields near Dubai.

Introduction

IN THE EARLY HOURS OF THE FINAL DAY OF MY last photographic trip to Dubai my daughter, Eloise, arrived at Dubai International Airport and was driven through the night to Al Maha Desert Resort & Spa so that I could photograph her for a fashion feature. She arrived before dawn just in time for our first shot.

Some time later, disappointed that she had to fly straight home that night and would not be able to see or experience anything of Dubai other than its airport and Al Maha, she asked me to describe the city.

This was a difficult question. Dubai is unlike any other place that I've visited and there was so much I could say and so many characteristics to describe that I found it difficult to answer her. Indeed, after several visits to this particular emirate, I may have had the photographs for this book but I still felt I wanted to get to know the city better and was planning further working trips to the UAE and a return visit to Dubai on a family holiday.

Dubai is always something of an enigma even for those who feel they know it well.

I have been coming to Dubai for some 30 years, the first time in 1976 when it was little more than a small settlement on a creek with one reasonable hotel. In the intervening years the change has been meteoric and it has been a fascinating exercise to observe its development from small trading post to a destination in its own right. I feel particularly privileged to have witnessed the change as I have always been attracted by the sights, sounds and smells of the Arab World.

My first visit to the Middle East was as small boy in the late 1940s when I flew out with my sister in a BOAC Hermes to Tripoli, in Libya, to visit our father who was then an officer in the Grenadier Guards. I can well remember the braying of the donkeys, the smell of dung, the squeak of the pumps, picnics in the ruins of Leptis Magna, trips into the desert to Gharyan and Yafran, and the excitement of a culture where Arab, Southern Mediterranean and African strands all came together.

On our first day we went to the local market to buy a donkey that I then shamefully tethered to my sister. In revenge she bet me her entire pocket money that I couldn't eat every fig off a tree in our garden, resulting in a short spell in

In the mid-1960s, to win a bet, I travelled from England to Kabul and back in my Mini Moke.

the Tripoli Military Hospital. Ten years later, in 1959, I went back to Tripoli, like my father, an officer in the Grenadier Guards, and participated in an endurance exercise through the desert from Tobruk to El Adem, marching some 100 miles in four nights.

My mother was instrumental in my next experience of travel in the Arab World. Worried that I might become too entranced by London in the 60s she bet me £100 in 1964 (then a considerable amount) that I couldn't get to Kabul and back without spending one night under a roof.

I set off with an old school friend, planning to follow part of Alexander the Great's footsteps, in my prized Mini Moke and a shared tent, travelling through Europe to Istanbul, down the coast of Turkey into Syria, where we explored the Crusader castle Krak des Chevaliers. In Jordan we visited Wadi Rum and Petra

before continuing our journey to Afghanistan.

In a journey of 50 days we endured 42 punctures as most of our driving took place on dirt tracks and rudimentary roads. We rarely found spoken English but encountered enormous hospitality along our route. Faithful to my mother's strictures we slept out every night which, in the Middle East, often meant that we strayed into tribal territory when pitching our tent. I soon found that a smile was the best disarming tactic when explaining our encroachment, a lesson that I've never forgotten and one that has even stood me in good stead when gaining access to such rarified areas as the last tee of the Dubai Desert Classic!

In Jordan we were not so lucky one night when we decided to camp a few miles off the main track. In the middle of the night my long-suffering friend nudged me awake, telling me to look up. Seeing a night sky filled with stars it became apparent that the tent had been stolen from over our heads while we were fast asleep. We found a replacement in Jordan and carried on regardless, accomplishing our objective and returning to London to claim the £100.

The expedition was a milestone in my growing-up process and also taught me about photography away from a controlled environment. I had an unsophisticated rangefinder camera, a light meter and a few packs of film, and struggled to capture the high-contrast images that the Middle East afforded me.

A few years later in 1967, now a fully-fledged professional photographer, I was sent on an assignment to Riyadh to photograph King Faisal.

His ascetic, hawk-like face was a photographer's dream. The city's first modern

Sheikh Zayed Road and the Dubai World Trade Centre photographed in the early 1980s.

buildings were then going up and I was expected to share the national enthusiasm in photographing this new architecture which I found not nearly as interesting as the traces of old Arabia. At that time I also visited Bahrain to photograph members of the royal family and enjoyed occasional fashion assignments to the Lebanon – always a welcome location.

One of the things absent on those early travels, except possibly in Beirut with its potent combination of Arab and French culture, was a level of what Westerners would call 'sophistication'. The first air-conditioned building I saw was in Dubai. This was not something I came across in my childhood, the army or during my early travels in the Middle East. On top of this, basic comforts such as reliable electricity, running water and decent restaurants were not to be expected.

THE TRANSFORMATION THAT IS NOW APPARENT IN Dubai has been phenomenal. Many of those who have never visited Dubai imagine it to be a kind of concrete jungle or artificial wonderland built with new money and having no character. This is not the case. The finance is certainly in place but there also appears to be a master-hand at work, assisted by dedicated experts and specialists. New developments of the type that other cities would see only once or twice every decade, or perhaps even once in a lifetime, seem to be announced daily in Dubai. Fantasies are translated into working reality.

The Burj Al Arab, for instance, has become as iconic a building as the Sydney Opera House. On first appearances it seems to belong to a Las Vegas setting with its fairy-tale entrance of dancing waters and underwater landscapes; gaudiness would seem to be the undernote.

My aerial view, from the opposite direction, of the same road in 2005.

Very soon one realizes that this is not just a first-class hotel but a majesterial one in a class of its own. In every area it excels and staying there is an experience never to be forgotten. But this is only one of several extraordinary hotels that Dubai has to offer as an adventure to the eager traveller.

Being passionately interested in food I am always overcome with admiration at the wealth and variety of restaurants that all these hotels have to offer. In the Madinat Jumeirah complex of several linked hotels, one can eat from no less than 31 different restaurants (excluding bars that also serve food and fast-food outlets) all with their different cuisine, be it Arab, Thai, Chinese, Italian, Californian, Spanish, all with the freshest ingredients flown in daily from every corner of the globe. I cannot think of anywhere else in the world remotely like this.

Another obvious example of getting things right is the constantly expanding and efficient airport which in 2004 served nearly 22-million passengers, with figures that are ever-increasing. Dubai's own airline, Emirates, has an international reputation and is constantly winning award after award in the travel business. Rather than following standards it is now setting them.

When I first came to Dubai I was surprised by the variety of nationalities that had come to work and live in the city as I had been expecting a predominance of UAE nationals. It reminded me of an assignment that I had for *Vogue* in the 60s when I was asked to photograph the great yachts of the world. I discovered what I thought was the perfect one, owned by a man called Charles Revson who owned Revlon.

The yacht was called *Ultima II*, the name of one of Revlon's cosmetic ranges, and Charles Revson had chosen each member of the crew to do the task that best suited their capabilities and talent. The engineers were Italian and German, the doctor Scottish, deckhands Filipino, laundry staff Chinese and so the list went on. Needless to say everything was perfection.

You experience the same thing in Dubai. Here you can find between 40 and 50 different nationalities working in one hotel and this gives you an idea of the cosmopolitan nature of the place. The fact that only 20 per cent of the population is comprised of UAE Nationals would seem to belie its essentially Arab feeling. It is surprising that, with such a small Arab percentage of the population, Dubai retains the integrity of a Middle Eastern country.

There is a strong feeling of hierarchy and structure that has a bearing on the way things work and explains why standards are so high. All too often one sees in other countries goals that are never achieved and projects started that are never completed. In Dubai things borne out of fantasy seem to reach fruition. We are now seeing the realization of The Palm Island projects, The World, already on target, the new Dubai Waterfront, the tallest building in the world and the largest shopping malls. Bold new projects are announced daily and they all promise to be successful. Even the tourists seem to be a cut above the average; none of the loutish behaviour and hooliganism that seems to blight Mediterreanean resorts. Perhaps they would not be tolerated.

I'VE ESPECIALLY ENJOYED WORKING ON THE PHOTO-graphy for this book because it has given me a chance to exercise my skills in every area of my profession. I've never wanted to be restricted to a particular branch of the industry and therefore become pigeonholed. I initially worked as a junior news photographer on a newspaper and then went on to assist a food and still-life expert so I learned the ins and outs of that very precise and quite different type of photography. From there I progressed to magazine work where I was involved in general photography, which is what I like to do best. I then went on to *Vogue* and was hired to shoot beauty and fashion. For a long time I concentrated mostly on fashion photography before getting back into portraiture.

Those of us who are truly interested in photography want to go out with an SLR and shoot from the hip. Luck and a good eye are essential. A quick reaction can produce what most photographers dream of – a candid image that records 'the decisive moment'.

Working on this book allowed me to use all those skills. My assistants and I travel with a full selection of cameras and are able to tackle more or less anything that is thrown at us (other than very specialized assignments, such as architectural photography, which requires particular equipment). We travel with a battery of lights, medium-format cameras, capable of grabbing more than 20-million-pixel digital images, and lightweight Olympus SLR digital cameras with both long and wide lenses so that we can cover almost anything. The joy of digital photography is that you don't have to change film all the time and you can adjust for the light and shoot in almost any circumstance.

This book has given me a wonderful chance to shoot portraits, landscapes, cityscapes, wildlife, fashion, sport and even food. I've been able to test a full range of capabilities and this is always challenging. For instance, I've always had a hankering to get back to landscapes and am very influenced by the work of the wonderful landscape photographers such as Ansel

Adams. I avidly purchase and study photographic books and one of my prized possessions is a signed and dedicated landscape print by the incomparable Henri Cartier-Bresson. Dubai also gave me a chance to do some aerial photography as I needed a bird's eye view of

With my daughter, Eloise, and the result of our work at Al Maha Desert Resort & Spa.

Working with my assistants, Iain Lewis and Kate Shortt, in the bustling area of Karama.

the city. We had to leave this as our last project, given how quickly things change in Dubai. It was fascinating to see The Palm projects that are taking shape so quickly.

I WOULD CERTAINLY RECOMMEND DUBAI TO other photographers. It is sensational as it offers just about every opportunity to shoot in any area and is a multi-faceted destination for photographers who want to try their hand at almost anything. Visually and photographically, Dubai's biggest highlight is the contrast in so many situations, including the juxtaposition of the desert with sophisticated high-rise buildings. The city is right on the edge of the desert and the Sheikh Zayed Road skyline provides a backdrop for many of the less urban photographs I took, from cricket and racing, to activities on the water and in the village markets. It always amazes me how much activity takes place right against the 'walls' of the city.

The shots in this book I'm probably happiest with are the ones that appear not to have been manufactured and posed and look natural and spontaneous, even though a lot of hard work might have gone into them. The Noodle House photograph (pages 148/9) is an example of this.

Another opportunity I enjoyed was a chance shot we grabbed from the side of the road with our small cameras and then decided to bring out the heavy artillery to go for a high-quality shot because I saw it as a possible exhibition print. This was a shot of a team of labourers in a weekend 'India versus Pakistan' cricket match on a rudimentary pitch on the desert *sabkha* (salt flats) with the Sheikh Zayed Road skyline as a background (pages 106/7). This was rewarding as it was a snatched moment that happened to work.

The desert landscape (pages 180/1) is in itself a wonderful exercise in graphics. Anyone teaching photography would have a field day experimenting with composition because, essentially, there are no rules. Everyone has a different eye and that is what makes it exciting and unpredictable. Either you have it in you or you don't.

The same could be said for city architecture (pages 70/1) where, in contrast to the desert, the powerful man-made structures create other disciplines of composition. Much of photography is about discipline, both in keeping up with technical advances and physically observing the unfriendly hours that 'catching the right light' demands. We're often up well before the sun comes up and finish long after it sets.

I've photographed people all over the world in unstaged impromptu situations but I've seldom found people as willing to be photographed as in Dubai. In fact it was quite difficult to stop people smiling. We received a very agreeable reception when we photographed a group of men in a *majlis*, relaxed and drinking tea and coffee (pages 52/3). Indeed, all the local inhabitants we photographed in the souks, *abras*, dhow-building yards, cricket grounds and other places were only too helpful and made things extremely easy for us.

I love hotel life in general and I was trying to analyse why I found it so impressive in Dubai and realised it was partly because I am so fond of good food. Eating in hotel restaurants when they are superb is always a happy experience and we decided, on the spur of the moment, to photograph a particularly beautiful presentation of food at a restaurant called Vu's in Emirates Towers. We shot four dishes in open daylight and arranged them vertically in a graphic presentation (pages 152/3) which gave us images that were entirely unplanned and, I hope did credit to a superb kitchen.

Another bonus in this assignment was that our trips were planned to coincide with sporting highlights in Dubai's calendar. We started in 2004 with the Dubai World Cup, the world's richest horse race (pages 112–121) that has the fashion, excitement and all that Royal Ascot has to offer. We went on to the tennis championships, another world-class event in every respect and won by the leading players in both the mens' and womens' rankings, Roger Federer and Lindsay Davenport, followed by

the Dubai Desert Classic which was won by the number one golfer in Europe at the time, Ernie Els. We enjoyed ad hoc cricket at different levels and the Dubai Rugby 7s, a great occasion made all the more enjoyable, for me, being won by England.

Glamour is in abundance in Dubai: glamorous events, glamorous cars, glamorous women from every area of life. I was privileged to photograph one notable businesswoman (pages 31–33) in her traditional *abaya* and *shayla*. This provided an interesting contrast from the fashion photography I've worked on for *Emirates Woman* magazine using models from Eastern Europe, Australia and London (pages 134–139). Another picture I like very much is a row of Emirates Airline stewardesses who seem to grace every major sporting event and are immensely photogenic. At the Dubai World Cup the women who stood out for their style and bearing were the Somalis who, with less worldly possessions than others present, had a natural elegance that was awe-inspiring and photographically challenging (page 116).

THIS, THEN, IS MY PORTRAIT OF A DYNAMIC AND colourful city that is easier to describe in photographs than words. The shots were taken during visits to Dubai during key events over one year and, since the face of the city changes so rapidly, this can only be a personal record of how Dubai looked during that short period.

It is my hope that those reading this book will enjoy it as much as I have enjoyed photographing it and, to return to Eloise and the beginning of this introduction, I hope it will show you the Dubai you never saw. . . .

Editor's note

Patrick Lichfield died unexpectedly in November 2005. His sudden death – shortly after completing this book – was a huge shock to many people, not least to us at Motivate Publishing who had worked on *Dubai – A City Portrait* with him.

PREVIOUS SPREAD: *His Highness Sheikh Maktoum bin Rashid Al Maktoum, Vice-President and Prime Minister of the UAE and Ruler of Dubai.*

LEFT: *His Highness General Sheikh Mohammed bin Rashid Al Maktoum, Crown Prince of Dubai and UAE Minister of Defence.*

The Dubai Creek is the focal point of the city as well as its main water-borne hub.

19

Dusk provides the best light to photograph buildings, in this case, the National Bank of Dubai, taken from an abra *(water taxi) on the Creek. The abstract shows our reflection in the curved windows of the bank.*

ABOVE: *The Creek attracts tourists of all nationalities who come to stroll along its walkways and shop in its souks.*

RIGHT: *Harking back to the days of maritime trade, the Textile Souk, Spice Souk, Gold Souk and Fish Souk are all conveniently situated adjacent to the Creek. Although motors have now replaced the lateen sail, I soon discovered there is no better place in Dubai to step back in time than along the Creek.*

*These dhows seen from our helicopter – and in the reflection
of the Twin Towers building – may look somewhat crowded
but are just a small part of the total number moored along the
Creek. Dubai has always been a trading centre and it was
trading and, later, the discovery of oil, that saved the emirate
from ruin when the pearling industry collapsed.*

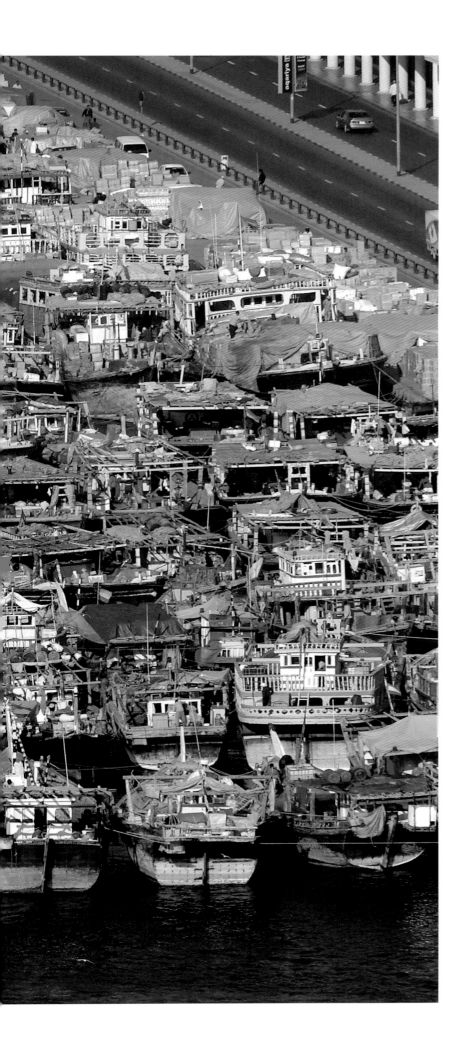

The trading dhows seen here and overleaf are, of course, home to their crews and still travel considerable distances with their varied cargoes. Throughout our visits to Dubai the crews always seemed to be making the best of the difficult conditions they live in. On another note, the picture on the left struck me as a wonderful subject for a jigsaw puzzle.

The Twin Towers are two of the more spectacular buildings on the Creek and home to the impressive Dubai Press Club, which enjoys a wonderful view of the Creek. At the club I photographed its General Manager, Mona Al Merri (above and following spread), a graduate of the Mohammed bin Rashid Programme for Leadership Development and widely recognised as one of the 'Young Leaders' of the city.

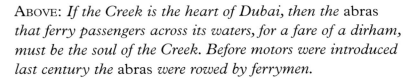

ABOVE: *If the Creek is the heart of Dubai, then the* abras *that ferry passengers across its waters, for a fare of a dirham, must be the soul of the Creek. Before motors were introduced last century the* abras *were rowed by ferrymen.*

RIGHT: *You can hire an* abra *for an intriguing tour of the Creek and prices are negotiable – especially during the quieter hours of the day. Mohammed Ahmed, the ferryman in the foreground of this photograph, hails from Iran and has been living in Dubai for 35 years.*

Higher up on the Creek, a team of oarsmen head out shortly after dawn for some exercise in their traditional rowing dhow while a wake-boarder enjoys a perfect winter's day with the tall buildings of Sheikh Zayed Road – Dubai's modern business district – forming a distant backdrop.

Saleh Al Geziry (left and previous spread) has a passion for horses and falconry and enjoys nothing more than combining these activities when not at work. Visitors to Dubai can themselves enjoy falconry and camels among the rolling dunes at the Al Maha Desert Resort & Spa (above).

Much of Dubai's heritage is celebrated at the Heritage & Diving Village, situated near the mouth of the Creek in Al Shindagha. Here, residents and visitors can enjoy a glimpse of Dubai's traditional culture and lifestyle. This shot of dhows was taken on my first visit to the pearl-diving area.

In Dubai I was fortunate to come across Humaid Ali Alrezi, a Bedouin who still has the habit of standing on one foot while leaning against his stick. This is one of my favourite shots in the book.

ABOVE: *This woman, wearing an* abaya *and a mask known as a* burqa, *allowed me to photograph her while she was preparing pancakes. When eaten with honey, the pancakes were delicious.*

LEFT: *A blacksmith, immersed in his work during the cooler evening hours, made another glorious subject.*

ABOVE: *As the day draws to a close, these men enjoy food, coffee and good companionship while discussing recent events.*

RIGHT: *Even in one of the most modern cities in the world, traditional dancing and music remain an integral part of the Arab culture and a favourite way to celebrate.*

LEFT: *Many of the old merchant houses of Bastikiya – the former merchant area of Dubai – have been lovingly restored.*

BELOW: *In Bastikiya I found examples of traditional architecture including windtowers, mosques and houses built round a central courtyard with every room opening on to it . . . this example houses the popular Majlis Gallery.*

LEFT: *While wandering around Bastikiya one evening, we were invited into a* majlis *(meeting place) for tea and captured this image of, seated from left, Yousef Mohammed Sharif, Yousef Mohammed Shaneef, Abdul Rahman Bastaki, Younis Abdul Khaleq Bastaki and Ahmed Adulla Abdul Majeed.*

ABOVE: *Inside the* majlis, *Yousef Mohammed Shaneef points to his family home in an historical photograph of Bastikiya.*

Wherever you are in Dubai, you will never be far from a mosque and the call of the muezzin. The image (previous spread) was taken in Bastikiya, while the mosque featured on these two pages, where tours are organised by the Sheikh Mohammed Centre for Cultural Understanding, is the well-known and much photographed Jumeirah Mosque.

Whether in the city or exploring ruins deep in the interior I was always on the lookout for traditional doors to photograph.

LEFT: *Windtowers, a natural form of air-conditioning, were introduced to Dubai by Persian traders who settled in Bastikiya in the early 1900s. The square towers are divided diagonally to form four triangular shafts which catch any passing breeze, push it down the tower and suck it up again, creating a welcome draught in the interior of the building. Although windtowers are no longer necessary in this modern age, they are still widely used as an architectural feature – and nowhere more spectacularly than at Madinat Jumeirah, which is featured in this pair of photographs.*

PREVIOUS SPREAD: *Another Arabian tradition is the* shisha *café. The water pipe – also known as a* hookah *or* hubbly-bubbly, *but more correctly a* nargile *– is smoked with a variety of aromatic flavours and is said to be even smoother than cigar smoking.*

RIGHT: *A view of Sheikh Zayed Road in 2005. With the face of the city changing at such a rapid pace, it's important to date photographs like this. Emirates Towers, currently the tallest building in Europe and the Middle East, is conspicuous near the top right-hand corner of the photo.*

FOLLOWING SPREAD: *Inside Emirates Towers, Mohammed Al Gergawi, Chief Executive Officer of the Dubai Holding company, in his office which boasts spectacular views of the city.*

No one has ever accused Dubai of having boring architecture and one of the most interesting buildings along Sheikh Zayed Road is the Dusit Dubai. This hotel marked the entry of the Thai-based Dusit hotel group into the Middle East in 2001.

*With its excellent accommodation, conference and exhibition
facilities, Dubai has come of age as an important meetings,
conferences and exhibitions destination, attracting top speakers
from both the Arab and the Western worlds. Pictured here are
Dubai's General Sheikh Mohammed bin Rashid Al Maktoum
(right top) and Rudolph Giulani KBE, former Mayor of New
York and* Time *magazine's 'Person of the Year', speaking at the
Dubai International Convention Centre off Sheikh Zayed
Road (right bottom). In the photo above, Sheikh Mohammed
is seen with Sheikh Ahmed bin Saeed Al Maktoum, President
of the Department of Civil Aviation, on his left; and German
Chancellor Gerhard Schroeder and Sheikh Abdullah bin Zayed
Al Nahyan, the UAE Minister of Information and Culture.*

PREVIOUS SPREAD: *Dubai Marina is comparable to the most exclusive waterfront developments in the world. Strategically located adjacent to Sheikh Zayed Road, it is one of Dubai's major developments and growing rapidly – there will eventually be 100 towers similar to the ones in this photograph.*

RIGHT: *One of Dubai Marina's first residents was comedian Jim Davidson OBE, seen here with his partner Michelle.*

ABOVE: *As this shows, Jim has a perfect view of the Emirates Golf Club from his balcony and often enjoys a game at the club.*

Most of the photography in this book was taken during the course of a single year and the construction I saw during that time was phenomenal. Jumeirah Beach Residence (left) and The Palm Jumeirah, seen behind a section of Dubai Marina (above), are just two of Dubai's numerous mega developments.

This view of The Palm Jumeirah may give you some idea of the magnitude of the task, even though it's the smallest of three similar islands, the other two being the Palm Jebel Ali and the much larger Palm Deira. There is also The World, a cluster of islands shaped, not surprisingly, like the world. I inspected Palm Jumeirah with Sultan Ahmed bin Sulayem, Chairman of Nakheel, the developers of all these man-made islands (above).

PREVIOUS SPREAD: *Emirates is one of the fastest-growing airlines in the world, but how do you say this in a photograph? We woke up well before dawn and shot this image at Dubai International Airport.*

RIGHT: *One of the first people to sit for me when I started work on this book was the charismatic Chairman of the airline, HH Sheikh Ahmed bin Saeed Al Maktoum.*

ABOVE: *Emirates is also well known for its cabin staff who add a cosmopolitan touch of glamour to many high-profile events, both in Dubai and around the world.*

RIGHT: *Maurice Flanagan CBE became Managing Director of Emirates when the airline began operations in 1985 and became Vice Chairman and Group President in 2003. "Emirates is owned by the Government of Dubai," he told me over lunch one day, "but we receive no subsidies. We have to be market-driven to survive, winning passengers and cargo customers the old-fashioned way . . . one at a time."*

Growing hand in hand with Dubai International Airport is Dubai Duty Free. From its launch in the closing days of 1983, Dubai Duty Free has matured into a company with an annual turnover of more than US$ 500 million (Dhs 1.8 billion) and is now widely recognised as one of the top airport-retail operations in the world. The Porsche in the foreground is one of the prizes in the 'Finest Surprise' promotion that has captured the imagination of the public.

ABOVE AND FOLLOWING SPREAD: *Dubai provides employment for many people from many countries – all of whom come to the emirate to better their prospects, and therefore have an impressive work ethic. Understandably, the booming construction industry is one of the major employers of labour and many of these men are recruited from the Indian subcontinent.*

Not all construction work is high tech. This man was photo-graphed working on a new villa at The Lakes, where the developer, Emaar, has constructed an attractive gated community where it's possible to rent villas of varying sizes.

Emaar also constructs villas and apartments for sale on a freehold basis, such as in The Springs (foreground) and, in the background, Dubai Marina. Other communities in this area include Emirates Hills and The Meadows.

Five years ago this area consisted of nothing but sand, now it provides some very attractive residential and holiday-home investments. On the left are the Springs and Meadows communities, on the right, Jumeirah Islands.

I visited this area several times in the hope of catching a perfect sunset silhouetting construction work at Dubai Marina and ended up with an image that also gives some idea of the scale of building going on in Dubai.

ABOVE: *There are more than 10 million Sikhs around the world, most of whom live in the Punjab although there are a fair number in United Arab Emirates too. The turban, beard and* kara *(steel bangle) are all distinctive.*

RIGHT: *This Punjabi man drives a massive excavator at a sand quarry deep in the heart of the desert.*

Ali Khalifa, television presenter and manager of the new-look Dubai TV, at work in the station's magnificent new studios in Dubai Media City – the new Middle East and global media hub.

ABOVE: *The Dubai TV studios broadcast out of Dubai Media City, in an area becoming known as the 'new Dubai'.*

LEFT: *Popular Dubai television producer and presenter, Shahnaz Pakravan, is well known not only in Dubai, where she has her own media production company at Dubai Media City, but also in Britain through her work with the BBC and ITN, including 'Arab World Direct' and 'Tomorrow's World'.*

Cricket is a popular game among the expatriates of Dubai and, on any winter's weekend, a number of matches are contested. A match that caught my attention (previous spread) was an impromptu test between Pakistan and India that we chanced upon on the sabkha near the top of the Creek, with the ubiquitous Sheikh Zayed Road skyline as a backdrop. Three members of the Pakistani team were Besmi Khan, Jamal and Jamshad Khan (left). We also saw formal games being played at Jaddaf, behind Al Wasl Hospital, where there are 15 sand-and-concrete pitches and two grass pitches, one of them floodlit.

Roger Federer completed a hat-trick of Dubai wins when he won the Dubai Duty Free Men's Open in 2005. The championships are held each year at the state-of-the-art Dubai Tennis Stadium.

Some of the world's best race horses congregate at the Nad Al Sheba Racecourse in Dubai each year for the Dubai World Cup, the world's richest horse race (previous spread). Synonymous with Nad Al Sheba and Dubai is the Godolphin stable which has achieved unparalleled success in international racing. It has always been associated with the best horses and jockeys, with Frankie Dettori (above) having ridden nearly 500 winners for the stable. Godolphin presently has some 350 horses in training.

Set in idyllic surroundings, Zabeel Racing Stables is one of the oldest and most prestigious stables in Dubai and is the private stables of HH Sheikh Mohammed bin Rashid Al Maktoum. Satish Seemar was recruited by Sheikh Mohammed in 1991 to set up and run the stables. He is seen at the stables in this photograph with his wife, Jacqueline, the Baroness von Hammerstein Loxten, and their daughter, Tara (right).

THIS SPREAD AND PREVIOUS SPREAD: *It's not just the horses that hog the limelight at Dubai World Cup in spring each year. As at any major horse race, anywhere in the world, you can see the latest in fashions, beautiful women and a kaleidoscope of colour and culture. In Dubai, even the children have a field day. . . .*

ABOVE: *Dubai's Nationals are always immaculately groomed and dressed but never more so than at the Dubai World Cup.*

LEFT: *The race attract numerous photographers, including Dubai's own 'Royal Photographer', Noor Ali Rashid, who has captured the history of the emirate for five decades and taken the photographs for a number of books on the subject.*

The Dubai Creek Golf & Yacht Club (previous spread) has recently been redeveloped and is the centrepiece of a resort that includes a hotel, villas, a marina and several restaurants, while the clubhouse (above) can be seen from many parts of the city. One of the newer championship courses in the emirate is The Montgomerie, Dubai (left), featuring 14 lakes, 72 bunkers and a signature hole with the largest single green in the world.

ABOVE: *The 'Big Easy', South African Ernie Els, clinched the 2005 Dubai Desert Classic at the Emirates Golf Club with a breathtaking eagle on the last hole, handing him an unprecedented third Desert Classic crown.*

RIGHT: *Enjoying themselves at the prize-giving that day were Sheikh Hamdan bin Mohammed bin Rashid Al Maktoum on the right and Mohammed Ali Alabbar, Director General of the Government of Dubai Department of Economic Development and Chairman of Emaar Properties.*

The Dubai Rugby 7s, the opening round of the IRB Sevens World Series, sponsored by Emirates, is not only a sporting spectacle but one of the biggest party weekends of the year. The December 2004 event held over three days was all the more satisfying because I was able to see my home country win, even if the photograph taken during the South Africa versus England semifinal (previous spread) tends to suggest otherwise!

Dubai is blessed with glorious, safe beaches where the water is clear, warm and inviting. There are popular public beaches such as those in Jumeirah (above) and beaches adjoining hotel properties including this impressive stretch fronting Madinat Jumeirah and The Jumeirah Beach Hotel (right).

In addition to this book, I've enjoyed a number of other Dubai assignments, including features for Emirates Woman *and* Hello! *magazines, portraiture and, of course, fashion — seen on this and the previous two spreads.*

RIGHT: *One of the most impressive features of Dubai – and one that I admire the most – is the exuberant display of flowers that greet you as you drive along the city's modern highways. I know of no other city that enjoys such lavish treatment.*

ABOVE: *Some residential areas, such as Emirates Hills, are also noticeable for their flowers, shrubs and palms, not to mention their verdant golf courses, while nurseries such as this one adjacent to Jumeirah Beach Road supply home owners with a wide variety of hardy plants for their gardens. . . .*

PREVIOUS SPREAD: *Even a long-time resident of Dubai cannot fail to marvel at the wonderful patches of landscaped greenery that are the parks of Dubai. One of the major attractions in Creek Park is Children's City, said to be the fifth-largest children's 'edutainment' centre in the world.*

*Dubai could justifiably be termed a 'shopping destination',
with many goods available at prices cheaper than in their
country of origin. New 'mega' malls are opening along Sheikh
Zayed Road and existing centres such as the upmarket
BurJuman (left) are constantly being enlarged and refurbished.
Nevertheless, for the time being, Deira City Centre (above)
appears to remain the city's most popular shopping destination.*

To many people, Dubai comes alive at night. This scene of Dubai Marina was photographed from Emirates Hills. On the right, a magnificent dome at the One&Only Royal Mirage welcomes guests and diners to the hotel.

ABOVE: *The award-winning Verre by Gordon Ramsay, situated in the Hilton Dubai Creek, is the three-star Michelin chef's only restaurant outside the United Kingdom. A number of other celebrity chefs also have plans to open restaurants in Dubai.*

PREVIOUS SPREAD AND LEFT: *The Noodle House, a contemporary South East Asian restaurant, is located in the Boulevard at Emirates Towers. Casual and affordable, this restaurant is one of my favourites, and I had great fun photographing it.*

Venison carpaccio with girolle mushrooms, baby asparagus and truffle vinaigrette.

Steamed halibut, baby artichoke and sunchoke purée.

Five-spice marinated wild duck with onion brûlée.

152

The challenge we set ourselves one afternoon when the weather and light were working against us, was to illustrate a complete meal in four images. Vu's restaurant rose to the challenge with dishes created by Nancy Kinchela and prepared by Praveen Kumar and Juraj Kalna. When not preparing food for photographers at short notice, Vu's serves modern European cuisine in a panoramic location on the 50th floor of Emirates Towers.

Thyme and yoghurt panacotta with mint jelly and melon juice.

At night some of the liveliest areas in Dubai are Satwa and Karama on the Bur Dubai side of the Creek and Al Sabkha in Deira. We spent an evening in Satwa, pausing at Ravi's – a Pakistani pavement café that's something of a local institution.

In addition to restaurants, cinemas and night clubs, there are a number of other night-time activities to choose from, including cultural evenings featuring Arabian and Western music. A highlight of the Shopping Festival in January and February is the Global Village with its numerous pavilions and amusement park. Dubai also attracts a number of leading pop stars and a Mark Knopfler concert coincided with one of my visits.

LEFT: *It is hardly surprising that Dubai attracts a number of celebrities, some of whom have homes in the emirate. One such person is Benazir Bhutto, former Prime Minister of Pakistan and the first woman to head an Islamic state.*

BELOW: *Seen at a premiere at the first Dubai International Film Festival is Orlando Bloom, star of the* Lord of The Rings *trilogy,* Pirates of the Carribean, *and a number of other films.*

I enjoyed exploring the old souks of the city, including the atmospheric Textile Souk in Bur Dubai and the Spice and Gold souks across the Creek in Deira. The stall keepers always have a smile and are more than willing to pose for an impromptu portrait while you discover where they come from – possibly Iran, India, Pakistan or Bangladesh. The most popular souk in Dubai must be the Gold Souk featured on this spread.

Since many of the authentic souks of Arabia have vanished with development it's not at all surprising that those that remain are as popular with locals as they are with tourists.

Souks don't necessarily have to be old and crumbling. Dubai's newest is Souk Madinat Jumeirah, which successfully recreates the atmosphere of an Arabian covered bazaar.

ABOVE: *A 'souk' with a difference is the Friday Market situated in the Hajar Mountains near Masafi on the road to the East Coast, where I captured this portrait of an Afghani rug seller.*

RIGHT: *The Textile or Cloth Souk faces onto the Creek adjacent to the main* abra *station in Bur Dubai. This is an old part of town with numerous small shops displaying colourful rolls of cloth and one stall even selling these finely embroidered shoes known as* mojris, *which are sometimes made from camel hide.*

The souks of Dubai, like those elsewhere in Arabia, are places to congregate, socialize and share opinions and news.

It seems that whatever souk you visit you will always find the ubiquitous watch stalls, while pashminas are also popular.

Although souks help to preserve many of the skills that make Arabian nations unique (above), we also found some unusual goods, mostly bank notes, coins and seashells, at this stall (right).

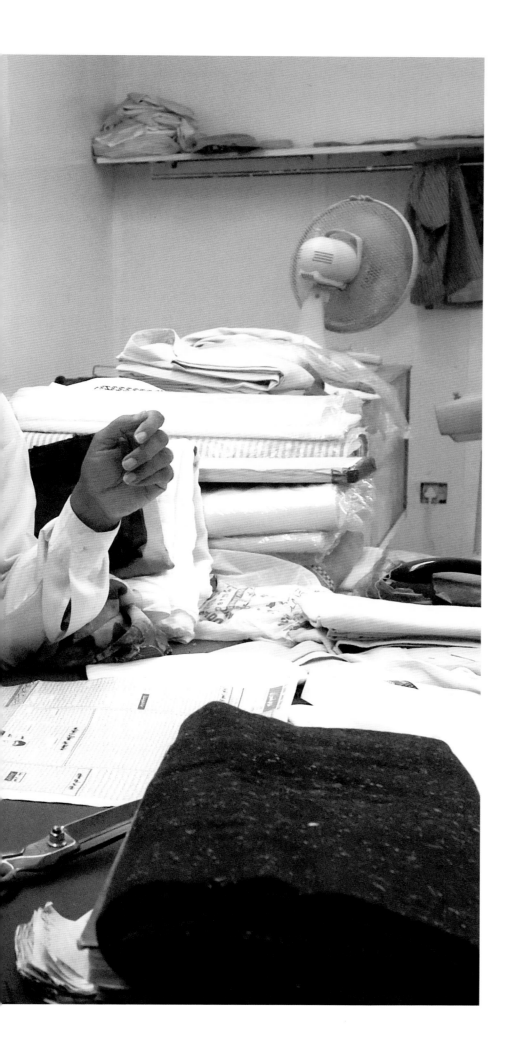

Not surprisingly, the Textile Souk is also home to a number of tailors' shops and I was rewarded with this portrait of an affable tailor in one of them.

A good-humoured Iranian stallholder in the Spice Souk. His shop is typically compact and caters for locals as well as the increasing number of tourists that visit the souk. Here you will find a selection of popular Arabian spices, such as cinnamon, rose petals and spices for curries. Look out also for incense (including frankincense), dried fruit and some delicious nuts.

A Pakistani labourer takes a break during the quieter afternoon hours (above). In addition to fish, a selection of fresh fruit and vegetables can be bought at the market in the Fish Souk (right).

Early one morning we found these fishermen offloading their catch right next to the Fish Souk, close to the mouth of the Creek. At the souk we found a huge choice of fish of various sizes, as well as a superb range of shellfish and even dried fish which made an interesting subject for an abstract composition.

There are some splendid areas within an hour's drive from Dubai, which are often at their best at sunrise. The road from Dubai to Hatta cuts through some pristine dune fields (above and following spread), as well as a number scarred by 4x4 tracks. A popular destination is Camel Rock (right), seen here with Fossil Rock in the background. You can motor up to the base of Fossil Rock and find a number of marine fossils – an indication that this area was once covered by the sea. I like to include a figure in landscapes to introduce a sense of scale.

ABOVE AND LEFT: *The dune fields and sandy wadis near Dubai are an inviting wilderness just waiting to be explored. They are not, however, a place for beginners or anyone travelling solo.*

PREVIOUS SPREAD: *Close to the Dubai–Hatta Road, and popular with local photographers, is a quarry where you can find remarkable sand patterns and even 'waterfalls' of sand.*

An umbrella thorn, Acacia tortilis, *reminiscent of the plains of Africa, on a lonely gravel plain near Hatta. The Hajar Mountains – the 'Backbone of Arabia' – form a spectacular backdrop.*

Stately old forts such as this one in the town of Bithna just beg to be photographed. Strategically located, this fort protected the route into the interior along Wadi Ham. It is surrounded by verdant date plantations and must be one of the most photogenic landscapes in the United Arab Emirates.

190

ABOVE: *Fujairah Fort, surrounded by the ruins of a crumbling mud-brick village, is arguably the most impressive of the forts of the UAE. It was bombarded by the British in 1925, the last time British gunboats opened fire in the Gulf of Oman.*

LEFT: *This weathered door was photographed at a fort near the village of Al Naslah, not far from the Omani border.*

The gravel road from Hatta to Al Ain winds through the Hajar Mountains, passing wadis, peaceful villages, small groves of date palms and natural swimming holes such as Hatta Pools. The minaret of the new mosque at the village of Ray may be seen from this road. This is an area where the people are traditional in their thinking and have strict social and moral codes.

A farm worker on the outskirts of Hatta. Encouraged by government funding and research, many suitable areas of the interior of the United Arab Emirates are under cultivation.

The Al Maha Desert Resort & Spa is run on similar lines to the private game lodges of Africa. In addition to luxurious chalets and a fine restaurant, guests can enjoy activities such as falconry, rides on camels and game viewing.

Al Maha, owned by Emirates, currently offers the best opportunities for viewing animals in their natural state in the UAE. Both sand and mountain gazelle occur in the 225 square kilometre Dubai Desert Conservation Reserve, in which Al Maha is situated, but they are difficult to differentiate in the wild, unlike the spiny-tailed lizard known locally as the dhub.

Gazelles are by far the most widely distributed genus and tribe of the antelopes, ranging from South Africa across Asia to Siberia and China. Seen here is a female with her offspring (left). Oryx also occur in Africa and Arabia, and the heraldic Arabian oryx (above) is the largest wild mammal at Al Maha.

The Ra's al-Khor Wildlfe Sanctuary is situated among the mangroves at the top end of Dubai Creek. It is a wonderful place to see flamingos, with hides to enjoy the spectacle.

The sanctuary attracts a number of other bird species and – while watching the flamingos – we were able to photograph this delightful pair of little green bee-eaters.

The colourful greater flamingos of Ra's al-Khor are the most conspicuous form of wildlife seen in and around Dubai.

Although greater flamingos are a common visitor to the large lagoons and mudflats of the Gulf during the winter months, some are present at all times of the year at Ra's al-Khor.

Acknowledgements

It requires the efforts and enthusiasm of a number of people and companies for a book such as *Dubai – A City Portrait* to see the light of day.

With this in mind, I should like to acknowledge the generous support and encouragement provided by the book's joint sponsors, Emirates airline and Jumeirah.

My gratitude also extends to Ian Fairservice and the rest of his team at Motivate Publishing, including David Steele, Andrea Willmore and Hazmit Concessao.

At Lichfield Studios I am indebted to Lady Annunziata Asquith, Iain Lewis, Kate Shortt, Penny Daly and Hatem and Peggy Farah.

I should also like to thank the people of Dubai for their willingness to pose – both formally and informally – for the book.

Photographic notes

In order to achieve the complex and diverse photographic subject matter featured within the book – ranging from aerial, architectural, fashion, portraiture and reportage to sport – a wide variety of photographic equipment was employed.

Our mainstay was the Olympus E-System (E-1 and E-300) with its comprehensive range of lenses. Although for specialised subjects we used the Hasselblad H1 Camera in conjunction with a PhaseOne P25 digital camera back.

All post-production was carried out in-house at Lichfield Studios. Retouching was done by Iain Lewis and proof prints were produced using an Epson Stylus Pro 4000 Printer.

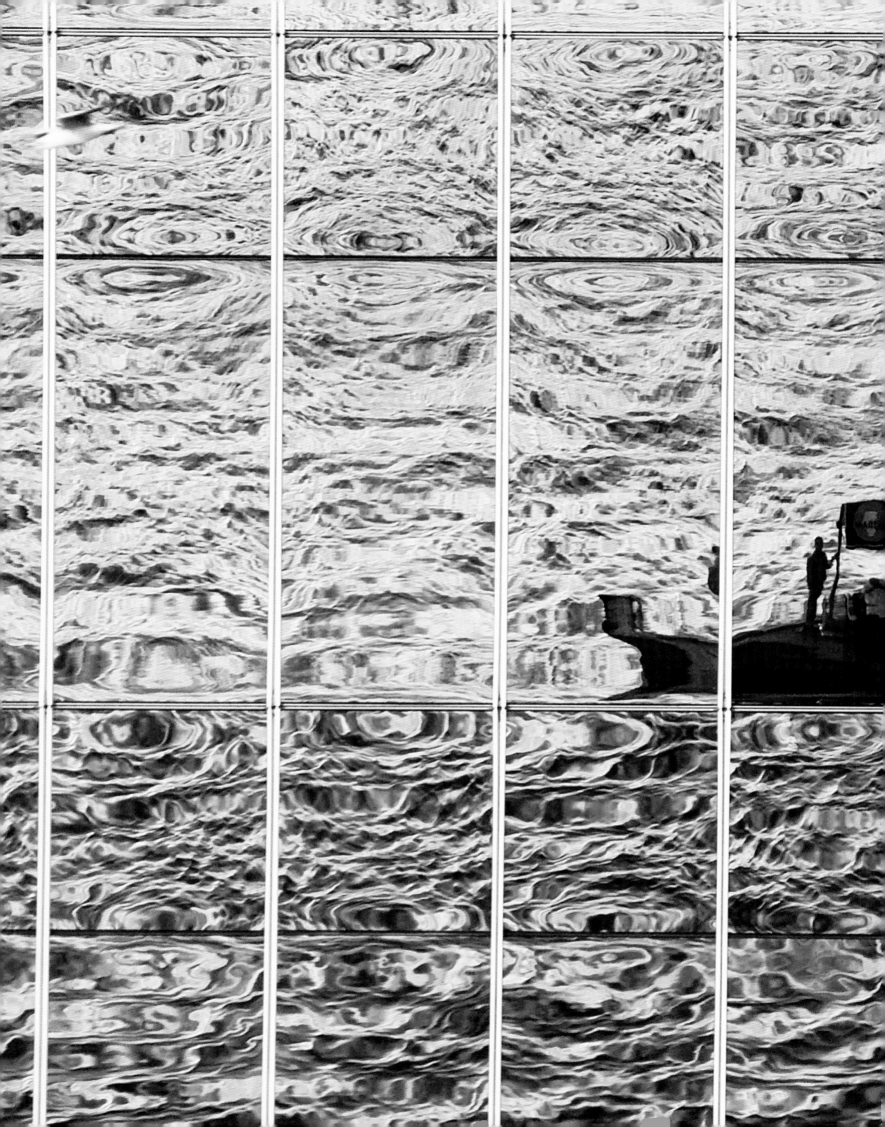